BUSINESS
SELLING
INSIGHTS

VOL. 5

BUSINESS SELLING INSIGHTS

VOL. 5

SPOTLIGHTS ON LEADING BUSINESS INTERMEDIARIES, BROKERS, AND M&A ADVISORS

FEATURING LEADING BUSINESS INTERMEDIARIES, BROKERS, AND M&A ADVISORS

Lee Sheaffer

Lisa Riley

Heather Valeri

Larry Fry

Michael Greene

Paul Semenoff

Philip Webb

Patrick Collins

Richard S. Waxman

Roxanne Reid

Business Selling Insights Vol. 5/ Mark Imperial —1st ed.

Managing Editor/ Shannon Buritz

ISBN: 978-1-954757-22-6

Remarkable Press™

AUTISM KNOWS **NO BORDERS;**
FORTUNATELY NEITHER DO WE.®

The Global Autism Project 501(C)3 is a nonprofit organization that provides training to local individuals in evidence-based practice for individuals with autism.

The Global Autism Project believes that every child has the ability to learn, and their potential should not be limited by geographical bounds.

The Global Autism Project seeks to eliminate the disparity in service provision seen around the world by providing high-quality training to individuals providing services in their local community. This training is made sustainable through regular training trips and contiguous remote training.

You can learn more about the Global Autism Project and make direct donations by visiting **GlobalAutismProject.org.**

CONTENTS

A NOTE TO THE READER

Thank you for obtaining your copy of "BUSINESS SELLING INSIGHTS Vol. 5: Spotlights on Leading Business Intermediaries, Brokers, and M&A Advisors." This book was originally created as a series of live interviews on my business podcast; that's why it reads like a series of conversations, rather than a traditional book that talks at you.

My team and I have personally invited these professionals to share their knowledge because they have demonstrated that they are true advocates for the success of their clients and have shown their great ability to educate the public on the topic of buying and selling businesses.

I wanted you to feel as though the participants and I are talking with you, much like a close friend or relative, and felt that creating the material this way would make it easier for you to grasp the topics and put them to use quickly, rather than wading through hundreds of pages.

So relax, grab a pen and paper, take notes, and get ready to learn some fascinating insights from our Leading Business Intermediaries, Brokers, and M&A Advisors.

Warmest regards,

Mark Imperial
Publisher, Author, and Radio Personality

INTRODUCTION

"BUSINESS SELLING INSIGHTS Vol. 5: Spotlights on Leading Business Intermediaries, Brokers, and M&A Advisors" is a collaborative book series featuring leading professionals from across the country.

Remarkable Press™ would like to extend a heartfelt thank you to all participants who took the time to submit their chapter and offer their support in becoming ambassadors for this project.

100% of the royalties from this book's retail sales will be donated to the Global Autism Project. Should you want to make a direct donation, visit their website at GlobalAutismProject.org

LEE
SHEAFFER

CONVERSATION WITH LEE SHEAFFER

■ **Lee, you are the founder of BizReady, Inc. Tell us about your work and the people you help.**

Lee Sheaffer: My heart is with entrepreneurs. It takes a special kind of person to be an entrepreneur. I enjoy working with people trying to buy, build, and sell their businesses. There's so much more to it than just coming to the finish line and wanting to sell.

■ **How prepared are business owners when it comes time to sell?**

Lee Sheaffer: The sad truth is that most business owners have not done anything to prepare. And in many cases, 85% of their personal wealth is tied up in their business. They are so busy with the day-to-day of work, selling their products and services, and running the company that they don't pay any attention to what needs to be done to sell their business.

■ What is the value of working with a business intermediary like yourself?

Lee Sheaffer: Businesses sell for more money if their owner prepares for their sale. Plus, sellers don't realize how complicated the process of selling a business really is. It's extra hard if you're trying to run your business and go through the selling process simultaneously because the selling process is very distracting. The best thing is to get a team of people around you several years ahead of time. It can never be too early. It could be when you first start your business, but certainly several years before you exit. It would be best to begin to educate yourself about what the buyer will be looking for and what things you can control to make your business more valuable. When a person is ready to sell, they must have their business ready. The business needs to be saleable. But they also have to be emotionally and financially prepared for life after the business. Getting all of these things lined up is very important to a successful transition.

■ Are there any myths and misconceptions about selling a business?

Lee Sheaffer: The worst situation is when a seller has no idea whether their business will be attractive to a buyer or what it is worth. So many sellers approach retirement and selling their business with ideas that are just not founded in reality. It's very dangerous for them. Not many businesses actually come to the market; they either get shut down or passed on to others. And many that do make it to market never sell. So owners need to have a good idea of what their business is worth and what they will do after selling it.

Often there is confusion about the "multiple" used to value a business. If the multiple is 3, for example, is that three times revenue, three times earnings before taxes, three times cash flow, and what does that multiple include? Does it include inventory? Working capital?

Another myth is sellers think they can do it all on their own. They really need the help of an intermediary and other advisors like CPAs and attorneys. There are just too many pieces of the puzzle for a business owner to handle alone, especially when trying to run their business simultaneously.

Buyers and sellers are natural adversaries because a buyer must look at the business from the perspective of "How can I improve it? What are the weaknesses?" But a seller who has put their entire life into building the business can have a hard time hearing and considering things from the buyer's perspective. Having someone in the middle to balance that out and aid in communication is essential.

■ **You mentioned that many businesses that go to market never end up selling. What are the reasons for this?**

Lee Sheaffer: 30% of the businesses that go on the market have a fundamental disconnect in the value of the business between the buyer and the seller. You probably won't make a deal if you go to market with an unrealistic idea of what your business will sell for. Another 20% fall out during the due diligence process, usually resulting from the owner not properly preparing for the sale. Business owners can take control if they start preparing three to five years before they want to sell. That way, they can answer all of the potential buyer's questions.

■ **As we are coming out of a pandemic and experiencing the "Great Resignation," is it a good time to buy and sell businesses?**

Lee Sheaffer: It's been quite a ride. The number of businesses was cut dramatically by the pandemic, as 50% of businesses substantially declined their revenues from the pandemic. Another 25% experienced little to no effect. And the last 25% actually did better. So half the market went away. 75% of the market with sellers who had plans to sell and retire got deferred or eliminated. So the number of good businesses available went way down, while at the same time, the number of buyers discovering there was a world outside of corporate employment went up. Of course, when supply decreases and demand increases, prices go up. Complicating it even more, some of those businesses experienced the "Covid bump," and their revenue actually went up. There's a real question about those businesses as to whether it will be a permanent shift or if their increase in sales will drift off. So it makes it very hard as a buyer to know whether you're buying something that will continue successfully into the future.

■ Lee, what inspired you to get started in this field?

Lee Sheaffer: I have the heart and soul of an entrepreneur. I've always worked for myself, and I have a financial background. I've been in and out of many different businesses and seen so many successes and failures. When I see an entrepreneur trying to start a business, or an owner preparing for a sale, I don't want them to experience the pain of missing important steps. There are things that sellers can do to get ready for the sale and be in control. Buyers also need to know what they can do to make a business really take off once they obtain it. There are value drivers that make a business worth what it's worth. It's why one business is worth two times its earnings, and another is worth ten times its earnings. I get tremendous satisfaction from being a student of those drivers and helping sellers and buyers understand and take control of their business future.

■ Is there anything else you would like to share?

Lee Sheaffer: The most important thing is to have the right team of advisors you can communicate with. As far as business brokers are concerned, look for members of organizations like the International Business Brokers Association. They are constantly updated and trained and are given opportunities to interact with their peers. There's also a wonderful organization called The Value Builder. John Warrillow founded it. It's a tremendous resource for business owners. You can learn more about Value Builder on my website and the drivers that will enable business owners to take control of their future.

■ How can people find you, connect with you, and learn more?

Lee Sheaffer: My website is www.bizreadybrokers.com. You can email me at lee@bizreadyinc.com. I focus on California, where I am a licensed real estate broker. Many states require business brokers to be licensed real estate brokers as well. If I can't help you directly, I can always help connect you to the right people. Check-in, and I will get you pointed in the right direction.

LEE SHEAFFER

CA Broker DRE# 00689023

Founder

BizReady, Inc.

Lee Sheaffer is a Certified Business Intermediary, Certified Value Builder, and graduate from the proverbial school of hard knocks. Her passion is helping fellow entrepreneurs succeed in buying, building, and selling their businesses, all the while avoiding painful and costly mistakes.

Lee has spent more than 30 years working in, for, and with small businesses as an employee, manager, owner, and consultant. In 1997, after 15 years as a self-employed business owner, she began consulting with small businesses. She is known as a creative problem solver who makes complex issues easily understood.

Lee founded BizReady, Inc., a California business brokerage firm, in order to help business owners prepare themselves and their businesses for a successful sale. BizReady, Inc. focuses on growing its clients' businesses through education about value drivers that are statistically proven to make a business more saleable and valuable. Owning a valuable, smooth-running business is ideal, and owners in such a position will be ready and able to sell successfully when the time is right.

EMAIL:

lee@bizreadyinc.com

PHONE:

510-384-1046

WEBSITE:

https://bizreadybrokers.com/

FACEBOOK BUSINESS:

https://www.facebook.com/BizReady-Inc-109197620695670/

FACEBOOK PERSONAL:

https://www.facebook.com/lee.sheaffer.96/

LINKEDIN:

https://www.linkedin.com/in/bizready/

LISA
RILEY

CONVERSATION WITH LISA RILEY

■ **Lisa, you are the founder and president of Delta Business Advisors of Scottsdale, Arizona. Tell us about your work and the people you help.**

Lisa Riley: Like most business brokers and intermediaries, we focus on clients with cash flow. We look at business owners' financials and provide a complimentary, most probable sales price analysis for those selling at the Main Street or lower M&A level. We offer full valuations and appraisals for those selling at the M&A level. So we cover the whole gamut from consulting, figuring out where you are, if you can sell now, and if you can sell for the price you want. We ask questions like, "Is it time for you to sell now? Are you personally ready to sell? Can you take that identity off your hat? Is your business ready?"

■ What concerns do business owners have when they first reach out to you?

Lisa Riley: There are three primary reasons people come to us, the first two are positive, and the third contains those less than positive motivators. One, they're ready to retire. Two, they have something else they want to do. Three, they have a driving cause pushing them to sell - the dastardly Ds - divorce, disaster, death, or dissolution of the partnership.

But regardless of how they come, I would say only about one out of ten has actually thought about exiting their business or put a plan in place for more than a year. Over 70% have not even thought about it until they contact us and are either ready or forced to be ready by current circumstances.

The main concerns are: "What's my business worth? How long will it take? I don't want my employees or customers to know I'm selling. How does this work?"

When it comes to the dastardly Ds, the owner probably won't get what they want or need out of the sale of their business. But if the sale is happening for positive reasons, they still have time to work and get what they need. Many small business owners are not ready to sell because they're working on the day-to-day and growing their business. They're working on keeping it going. And if they're coming to us when it's in a downturn, buyers see that too, and they've lost the value. Buyers want to buy businesses going well, just like you want to keep your business when it's going well.

■ How far in advance should business owners prepare to sell?

Lisa Riley: We always say three to five years is ideal if you haven't started on day one of owning your company. Few owners have, but we run into some. In those three to five years, you should take month-long vacations and let your employees get used to handling the day-to-day operations. Take the time to get your financials cleaned up. Begin working out all of those perks; if you take a business trip and decide to bring your family and stay an extra two weeks, those things should begin to come out of your business financials. You will pay more in taxes in the short term, but it will increase the value of your business by two to seven times.

■ As we are coming out of a pandemic and experiencing the "Great Resignation," is it a good time to buy and sell businesses?

Lisa Riley: It depends on the industry, the type of business you want, and your skills. Buying a business is a risk. Selling a business is a risk. Life is a risk. But for example, accounting/bookkeeping is a buyer's market right now. We have a large number of baby boomers who are ready to retire. Less than three years ago, it was a seller's market; we were getting top dollar for accounting firms. Now more people want to sell in certain areas. On the other hand, it is a seller's market in most other areas such as manufacturing and construction. Any owner with a booming business, with good books and records, excellent employees, and a solid customer base is finding themselves in a seller's market.

■ **Statistics show that 80% of businesses on the market never sell. What are the reasons for this?**

Lisa Riley: The main one is the financials don't support what's being purported. In addition, the price that a buyer is willing to pay is not what a seller is willing to accept. There are lots of reasons for this one. An owner has a number in their head for their company valuation, which might be an accurate number. But it might not be for that type of buyer. For example, you would do a valuation for many reasons, including divorce, partnership dissolution, adding a partner, selling a business to a third party, or selling the business internally. The value will differ dramatically with each circumstance. If you're selling to a third party, the value will depend. Is it a financial buyer? Is it a strategic buyer? Is it a competitor? Is it an individual; can they get an SBA loan for businesses less than $5 million in sale price? So all of those things come into play.

Secondly, the financials have to be easily understood. And that means that the EBITDA (earnings before interest, taxes, depreciation, and amortization) has to be clear and can't have all of those adjustments like family trips, as discussed earlier. Sooner or later, the buyer says, "No, I'm just excluding it."

Lastly, the owner cannot be the key person who all decisions are made through. If this is the case, the buyer will lose that key person and potentially the entire business. The same would apply to customer concentration. If 90% of the company's revenue stream comes from selling to Costco, it would be tough for a buyer to swallow if Costco goes away.

■ Lisa, what inspired you to get started in this field?

Lisa Riley: The short, 20-second answer is I'm a sociologist by trade. I taught for ten years at a university. When I came to Arizona, we built our own house, and I was the general contractor (GC). To help others, I could either get my GC license or my real estate license. In Arizona, you must be a licensed real estate agent or broker to sell businesses. So when I discovered that I could help business owners as a business advisor, I was all in! I made this my primary focus because I have seen the good and the bad. A business is typically one of the largest, if not the largest, assets a business owner has. They get one chance to do it right and exit on their terms.

The 80% of businesses that never sell are primarily due to bad advice, bad records, or a fully owner-operated business. Nobody wants to buy a job for less than they would work for someone else.

- ## How can people find you, connect with you, and learn more?

Lisa Riley: Our website is www.deltabusinessadvisors.com. You can also email me at lisa@deltabusinessadvisors.com. My phone number is 480-686-9031.

LISA RILEY, PHD, CBI, CM&AP, CBB

Founder and President

Delta Business Advisors, LLC of Scottsdale, Arizona

Lisa Riley is the Principal of Delta Business Advisors. She and her team assist sellers and buyers in selling and purchasing their businesses.

As a current and former business owner, Lisa understands the demands and freedoms of both one's business and moving into the next phase in life. She and her team have assisted in hundreds of successful transitions by focusing on the wants and needs of their clients.

Lisa and her team stay up to date on industry trends. Her industry knowledge and an extensive network of business owners and intermediaries ensure business owners get maximum exposure when it comes time to sell or purchase a business.

She earned the designations of Certified Business Intermediary (CBI) from the International Business Brokers Association (IBBA) and Certified Mergers & Acquisitions Professional (CM&AP) from Coles College of Business- Kennesaw State University. Lisa was also awarded the prestigious Tom West Award.

Her educational achievements include a BA from Benedictine College (KS) and an M.A. and Ph.D. from the University of Notre Dame (IN). She is a member of various M&A industry associations, including M&A Source. Lisa is active in the industry, has served on the IBBA and the Arizona Business Brokers Association (AZBBA) boards, and is the past chair of both associations.

EMAIL:

Lisa@DeltaBusinessAdvisors.com

PHONE:

480-686-9031

WEBSITE:

www.DeltaBusinessAdvisors.com

LINKEDIN:

https://www.linkedin.com/in/rileylisa/

HEATHER
VALERI

CONVERSATION WITH HEATHER VALERI

■ **Heather, you are the President of Meridian Business Advisors, LLC. Tell us about your work and the people you help.**

Heather Valeri: I specialize in working with small business owners who earn $500K to $10 million a year in revenue. I prefer to work with highly motivated individuals who have a clear vision of what they want to do. My firm puts the clients first.

I will occasionally help a small business owner who is struggling because I think every small business owner should have a resource. I think of myself as an advocate first and then a business broker.

▪ What concerns do business owners have when they first reach out to you?

Heather Valeri: The common questions I get are, "What is my business worth? Will my competition find out my business is for sale? How long will this take? What does this mean for my employees? What does this mean for my family?"

▪ Do you find there is a lack of information about selling businesses?

Heather Valeri: 50% of businesses close due to unfortunate circumstances, poor planning, or lack of financial resources. 20% of those owners who shut their doors didn't even know selling their business was an option. So there is definitely a lack of education and information for small business owners. I like to walk them through the entire process and say, "Hey, this is what it looks like to sell your business." I always do a free, fair market valuation. If they want to do something more comprehensive, we can perform a business valuation to learn what the business is worth.

■ How far in advance should business owners prepare for selling?

Heather Valeri: As soon as you start building your business, you should think about your five-year and ten-year plans. When you write your business plan, you should also consider what your exit might look like down the road. Are you going to leave the business to family? Are you going to sell it and retire? It is best to put an exit plan in place from day one.

■ What advice do you give business owners to alleviate some of their concerns?

Heather Valeri: I always listen to my clients to get a feel for their top goals and concerns. We use this information to create a strategic plan for selling the business. Confidentiality is always my first priority. We market the business so that our client's competitors do not find out. We also do our best to ensure the employees still have jobs after the sale of the business.

■ What are common reasons for businesses being unsellable?

Heather Valeri: Unfortunately, all business brokers do not receive the same training. So that's one of the issues. People just say, "Hey,

I want to be a business broker today." And in their particular state, there may not be licensing requirements. So the process in itself is faulty.

Over 50% of businesses on the market do not sell on a national average. My company, however, has a 90% success sale rate. If you list with us, we will sell your business 90% of the time.

Businesses that don't sell don't have their books in order, or there's an inherent problem. So when I do a valuation of a business, I try to find out the strengths and the challenges. How can we market it better? What's the investment opportunity for other business owners? Why would they want to buy your struggling business? We get our clients top dollar for their business and property.

■ Heather, what inspired you to get started in this field?

Heather Valeri: I have a background in marketing, corporate mergers, and acquisitions. I came from a long line of business owners. Many people on both sides of my family went to college to be accountants. Some of them were excellent business owners, while some of them failed. I always thought education was the difference. As I got older and gained more real-world experience, I learned that education plays a role, but the real difference is made by character. A small business owner must have resolve, grit, resilience, and the commitment to succeed.

I know a gentleman who owns 26 ice cream businesses. I also knew a lady who owned one of these same businesses. And she did terribly, while the gentleman was doing very well. What was the difference? It was the same business model. But in this case, it was about the individual, their approach, and their desire to succeed. I want to be part of helping business owners succeed and create legacies for their families.

■ Is there anything else you would like to share?

Heather Valeri: If you are considering selling your business next year, get your house in order. Clean up your financials, update your employee handbook, branding, etc. The top priority needs to be having your financials accurate and image polished to get top dollar for your business. If not, we can work with business owners on a consulting basis to improve their value.

■ How can people find you, connect with you, and learn more?

Heather Valeri: I am on Facebook and Instagram at Meridian Biz Advisors. You can also go to either one of my websites: www.meridianballc.com or www.meridianfranchises.com.

HEATHER VALERI

President, Certified Business Intermediary
and Small Business Advocate

Meridian Business Advisors, LLC

Heather has been a small business broker for ten years and has worked in corporate mergers and acquisitions for over 15 years. She has consulted for global companies, Fortune 500, and medium to small businesses. She has worked in several industries, including technology, telecom, healthcare, finance, insurance, and retail. Heather is also an advocate for entrepreneurs and veteran business owners. She has been involved with several professional and civic organizations, including IBBA, CVBBA, Rotary International, SCORE, etc. She coaches minority business entrepreneurs through the Good Enterprises Program and founded a Veterans & Advocates Business Networking Group. She has earned several awards for her marketing expertise and contributions. Heather holds many certifications, including being a Certified Business Valuator and Certified Franchise Consultant and Developer.

EMAIL:
hvaleri@meridianballc.com

PHONE:
843-800-2148

WEBSITE:
www.meridianballc.com www.meridianfranchises.com

FACEBOOK:
https://www.facebook.com/MeridianBiz

INSTAGRAM:
https://www.instagram.com/MeridianBizAdvisors

LINKEDIN:
https://www.linkedin.com/in/heathervaleri

LARRY FRY

CONVERSATION WITH LARRY FRY

> ■ **Larry, you are a Senior Business Advisor with Transworld Business Advisors of College Station in Texas. Tell us about your work and the people you help.**

Larry Fry: Our territory encompasses nine counties, but our most prominent area is the Bryan-College Station area, home to Texas A&M University. We service small and medium-sized Main Street businesses, such as ice cream shops and liquor stores. Liquor stores are actually pretty popular, and one of the businesses deemed essential in Texas, so they were open during the pandemic, and we were still able to help sell them. Other popular businesses in our market are health clubs, spas, cryotherapy, and yoga studios. In addition, tech consultation is booming because of the university. It's a small metropolitan area, and many local businesses, such as restaurants and hotels, depend on Texas A&M University. Now that Covid is over and the university is open again, they are getting 100,000 people at the football games, and those businesses are doing well. So it's a very nice territory to cover.

■ How far in advance should owners prepare for the sale of their business?

Larry Fry: The business broker's current issue of the day is making sure your clients have an exit strategy in place all along. While starting and building the business, they need to have an exit strategy in mind to maximize the value as they operate. Then when they finally decide to sell, hopefully before something bad happens, they won't be scrambling to put all the pieces together to maximize value. Most business brokers will advise you to have an exit strategy in place from the very beginning. This would involve removing yourself from the business's daily operations and having a trusted manager or supervisor who will stay on after you sell. If all of the knowledge is in the business owner's head, they will lose value because there is nobody to hand the baton off to effectively. So we always tell owners to have an exit strategy in place from day one.

I read an article on the restaurant business sector the other day on www.bizbuysell.com. They recommend spending the first year establishing the business, creating menus, advertising, and getting people in to eat the cuisine. Then over the next three years, they recommend that you start building it up while having an exit strategy in place. Then during the fifth year, you either revamp with a new theme and new menus to entice and maintain your customer base, or you sell to a new owner who will do the revamp. So this represents an effective five-year exit strategy for a small to medium-sized restaurant.

Finally, many business owners don't have an effective exit strategy in place during the life cycle of their business, so when illness or death strikes, their families have no idea what to do with it. They then end up selling the business for pennies on the dollar. So this represents the most significant hazard of not having a good exit strategy during a business's life cycle.

■ What can an owner do to make their business attractive to a potential buyer?

Larry Fry: As stated previously, you must remove yourself from the daily operations. It would be best to have a solid team in place that could carry the baton forward once the business gets sold. You also need to have your books straight, so don't have your financial documents in a shoebox. It's nice to be audited yearly, have your tax records and Schedule Cs in place, and hopefully, all certified by a CPA or accountant. Having good books demonstrates that you ran the business effectively and kept it organized. Unfortunately, many small business owners don't use accountants; they write everything on paper and shove it in the proverbial shoebox, which makes the broker's job a lot harder and reduces the business's value when things fall through the cracks.

> ■ **As the pandemic is ending and we are experiencing the "Great Resignation," is this a good time to buy and sell businesses? What are you seeing in your market?**

Larry Fry: The problem in College Station is that businesses are booming again, but there is a significant shortage of able-bodied employees. Now that the local businesses are ramping up and getting busy again, their growth and profitability are being impeded by not being able to get enough workers in place to help with running the business. As a result, we are still playing catch up with the noted employment issues in College Station. So even though things are booming again, they could be even better with proper staffing. All the competent employees seemed to have disappeared during Covid, and nobody knows where they all went.

For example, I'm currently selling a custom framing and art gallery owned by a man and his wife, and at the consultation, he told me that one of the reasons they are selling is because they can't find employees. They have had it for over 30 years and are now ready to sell. But I still told them they needed to find and train a manager and a couple of employees to maximize the value of the business. So the remnants of Covid remain in these under-employment issues, but hopefully, that will start to go away soon.

■ Larry, what inspired you to get started in this field?

Larry Fry: I was a computer software developer/consultant in Houston for 36 years with major energy companies. When I turned 58, I said, "I'm tired. I'm done. I can't do this anymore." I knew the regional vice president of United Franchise Group here at the time, and we started going over franchises that I might want to acquire to start my own business. Then he recommended Transworld Business Advisors. I went to the discovery day at UFG's West Palm Beach office to discover another franchise they had in the offing, and I found Transworld Business Advisors while there. I then bought Transworld's College Station franchise in 2017 from a man who was retiring. I operated it as the Principal Broker for four years, having then sold it in September 2021 to a retired Exxon-Mobil employee. I am still heavily involved with the franchise as a Senior Business Advisor.

Business brokering is exciting and challenging at the same time. I really like it, and it's nice to be in a position to oversee all of the facets of closing a deal. I get all the requisite lawyers, accountants, and escrow officers together to close deals. My job is to manage the closing and ensure that all the proverbial ducks are in a row, which is the most challenging part of being a broker. My busiest times are during closings, and I have to keep all the cattle in the yard, so to speak, to prevent things from falling through.

■ How can people find you, connect
with you, and learn more?

Larry Fry: You can Google "Transworld Business Advisors of College Station." You will find me there on the website and all my contact information.

LARRY FRY, MBA

Senior Business Advisor

Transworld Business Advisors of College Station

As a Senior Business Advisor with Transworld Business Advisors of College Station, TX, Larry Fry has served as a senior-level business broker, intermediary, and advisory consultant covering the Brazos Valley region of Southeast Texas. He provides business brokerage, intermediary, and valuation services to both sellers and buyers of

Main Street businesses in the area. He partners with attorneys, accountants, business brokers, escrow agents, M&A advisors, private investors, and other professionals to provide these services to sellers and buyers of businesses in the region. Mr. Fry serves Brazos Valley counties, including Austin, Brazos, Burleson, Fayette, Grimes, Lee, Milam, Robertson, Waller, and Washington.

As a senior business broker/advisor, Mr. Fry strongly encourages all of his clients to seek the services of qualified attorneys, accountants, escrow agents, and/or other professional advisors when entering into the sale or purchase of a business. Also, if a prospective buyer wants to buy a good business with rock-solid fundamentals that will transaction well and can grow under their ownership, they must be prepared to pay a nice premium for it.

Sectors of Specialization: Alternative Wellness Spas; Art Galleries/ Framings; Automobile Services; Computer Software; Construction, eCommerce; Finance; Information Technology Managed Services; Mobile Food/Beverage Catering; Liquor Stores; B2B Signs Banners & Graphics; Nail Salons; Tanning Salons; Transportation.

EMAIL:

Lfry@tworld.com

PHONE:

+1 (979) 599-5200

WEBSITE:

College Station Business Brokers | Transworld Business Advisors (tworld.com)

LINKEDIN:

https://www.linkedin.com/in/larryfry

BIZBUYSELL:

Larry Fry, MBA Business Broker Profile - BizBuySell

FACEBOOK:

https://www.facebook.com/
TransworldBusinessAdvisorsCollegeStation

MICHAEL GREENE

CONVERSATION WITH MICHAEL GREENE

■ **Michael, you are the president of Sam Goldenberg and Associates and Sunbelt New Mexico Business Advisors. Tell us about your work and the people you help.**

Michael Greene: Sam Goldenberg and Associates has been around since 1983. Working in New Mexico, you pretty much have to be a generalist. I come from California, where I did mergers and acquisitions, and you can be very specialized there. In New Mexico, we work with all kinds of businesses covering the whole state. Our general size is between $500,000 and $5 million, with most listings in the $1 million to $4 million range.

■ **Are owners as experienced at selling businesses as they are at growing businesses?**

Michael Greene: No, probably not. We have an exit specialist on staff with extensive corporate America and national consulting backgrounds. If a company is not prepared for a successful sale, we will work with them for a year or however long it takes to get their procedures, processes, and books in the best condition possible to be more attractive to buyers. Often the sellers are not really in a position to sell; they've just reached a point in life where they'd *like* to sell.

■ **How far in advance should an owner prepare for the sale of their business?**

Michael Greene: It all depends on the type of business and how well it has been run. We see people ready and willing to sell now, anxious to sell for many reasons, and others who might need a year to put themselves in the proper position to sell. When they first reach out to a broker, they are looking for a better understanding of the process. What will it be like to sell their business? Can it be kept confidential? Confidentiality is a primary concern, as they don't want the world to know the business is for sale. Having the whole state makes it easier for us to cloak or camouflage a business.

From a business broker standpoint, things have changed significantly in the last 30 to 35 years. It's gone from a pioneer industry that was not well known or understood by mainstream brokerages to having intermediaries represent a significant part of the brokerage world. The true challenge of being an intermediary is working with the buyer and the seller simultaneously. It requires a tremendous amount of fairness and openness. We like to get testimonials from buyers and sellers that sound alike, where they both think we were fair and transparent and gave them all the information they needed to make decisions. That's the biggest difference between being a real estate broker or a lawyer, where you only work with one side. Here, you're working with both the buyer and the seller and trying to be fair to both. Great business brokers and intermediaries can do this consistently.

■ Statistics show that 80% of businesses that go to market never sell. What are the reasons for this?

Michael Greene: The breakdown starts at the very beginning when brokers are too anxious to take a business to market that isn't really sellable or too willing to let the seller dictate the terms of the sale. It shouldn't be that way. It's not that way for us. We are fortunate and blessed to be able to turn down sellers who aren't realistic or don't have an attractive business. We have a track record of selling everything we list. And I think that's how it should be.

One of the reasons I work with only staff and am the only actual broker is that I don't want people working for me who need to get a commission so badly they get themselves involved with a seller

LEADING BUSINESS INTERMEDIARIES, BROKERS, AND M&A ADVISORS

that is not realistic and, therefore, not going to succeed. I come from a background in commercial real estate as well. And that's always been one of the problems. So we're all staff; I'm the only one on commission and/or success fee, as we like to call it. And for that reason, my team can be realistic with the sellers about the value of the business. So the real problem is intermediaries who are so anxious to list businesses and make sales out of scarcity that they take on businesses that won't sell. There's no reason any business you take on shouldn't sell.

Some intermediaries also don't prepare enough collateral material. We spend two to three months from when you say you want us to sell your business to learn everything about your business and create truly professional collateral materials and a confidential business review. When buyers show up, they're confident they're getting the real information. If a buyer feels things are being withheld, they will not buy that business. All in all, the most successful brokerages, including ours, sell just about everything they list.

■ **As we are coming out of a pandemic and experiencing the "Great Resignation," is this a good time to buy or sell a business? What has the market been like in your area?**

Michael Greene: The market has been very strong due to the low interest rates and loans readily available to buy businesses. SBA loans have been readily available because the government has encouraged them. And most buyers need and want a loan no matter how much money they have. They tend not to buy things for cash; they borrow the money. So it's been a great market because the funds have been available at low interest rates, making it easier to buy a business for more money since your loan payment is less.

That's beginning to change. I think many people are selling right now because the pandemic has made doing business less pleasant and more frustrating. Ten years ago, we talked about baby boomers exiting the market and thousands of businesses going up for sale, but it didn't happen. Baby boomers kept working. They didn't quit at 65. Now, they are 75, and the pandemic makes running a business unattractive to them. So they're selling, and buyers have been anxious to buy because they sense there's an inflationary period coming where everything will become more valuable. Right now, I'd say the market is still extremely strong. But concerns are beginning to build like thunderclouds, so perhaps people will become more cautious about buying as they did in 2008 and 2009. But right now, I'd say it's a really excellent time to sell your business because bank loans are still available. When the loans go away, sellers are forced to finance, which is less attractive to them.

■ **Michael, what inspired you to get started in this field?**

Michael Greene: I think it's always about movement and professional growth. So I started in California as an attorney. I morphed into mergers and acquisitions, which were a huge deal 40 years ago. I came to New Mexico because I wanted to live here, and my wife is an artist who wanted to be in Santa Fe. Being here, I had to get more realistic about what was available. We don't have huge businesses here. I had Prudential agencies, which basically work with Fortune 100 companies. So when I came to New Mexico, I joined Sam Goldenberg and Associates because they were a pioneer in the intermediary field and had dominance in all of Northern and Central New Mexico.

Over the years, I've tried to keep up with the times and grow it into a statewide company. So we've morphed into this. It takes several skills. You need a legal background since there is a lot of documentation. It is also good to understand working with buyer and seller clients on both sides and have the ability to communicate clearly with people. You need to know a little bit about an awful lot of businesses, which you only get with time. So part of what makes a good intermediary like me is having done it for 25 or 30 years because you've run into every kind of business out there.

When I hire inexperienced new staff, they have to come to me with every different type of business to understand how it works. As time goes by, you develop those skills, making you a more successful and valuable intermediary because you understand the seller's business. You understand the kind of buyer that buys that type of business. The same buyer doesn't buy every type of business; there's a profile for those buyers as well.

So I like it because there's a lot of variety in it. And it isn't doing the same thing over and over again. It utilizes my skills and my personality. I believe whatever you do in life should fit your personality. Some personalities fit accountants; some personalities fit salespeople. And this is more sales than accounting. So sometimes someone can have a tremendous background in finance and have the personality of an accountant. But it's hard for them to have the conversations they need to make a buyer and seller comfortable in one of the biggest decisions of their lives. For most sellers, the business is the largest asset they have. And for most buyers, it is the biggest investment they're ever going to make. So there's a lot of fear on both sides that has to be smoothed and dealt with, and you can't ignore it; you have to dig in with them and have them understand exactly what's going on.

I've been doing this for so long that it's hard to remember when I *wasn't* a business intermediary. And to me, it's a pretty natural thing to be doing in a state like New Mexico. Living in a beautiful city like Santa Fe, I'm selling the lifestyle, venue, and location in large part. Working in a big city is different because you're mostly making lateral sales. If you want to sell a dry cleaner, you call dry cleaning companies because they want more market share. In a place like New Mexico, it's less about lateral sales and more about dealing with people who want to live in New Mexico or Southern Colorado, as we also work in Durango. They want to live here, and therefore they want to find something interesting to do. Often they've come here with money for a second career. And so it's a little different from Los Angeles, where I started. And I like it better that way. Often it's easier to sell a business here because the people want to be in Taos, they want to be in Santa Fe, they want to be in Albuquerque, they want to be in Las Cruces. And I just have to find the right hole for that peg. That's what we do. And we're very fortunate to do it well. In business brokerage, it's really all about the referral system. We have built Sam Goldenberg & Associates from personal referrals from businesses, accountants, and lawyers, and it takes a while to do that. But that's what makes a business brokerage firm like ours successful.

■ How can people find you, connect with you, and learn more?

Michael Greene: We have two websites: www.samgoldenberg.com and www.sunbelt.com. You can also Google "business broker in New Mexico, Santa Fe, or Albuquerque," and we will show up. You can reach me very easily. We have a large staff that takes the calls, and I'm always available to talk with anybody who thinks they could benefit from that conversation.

MICHAEL GREENE

President

Sam Goldenberg and Associates and Sunbelt
New Mexico Business Advisors

Since taking the helm of Sam Goldenberg & Associates in the mid-2000s, Michael Greene has grown it into a regional powerhouse and the Sunbelt Network's exclusive representative in New Mexico. Sam Goldenberg & Associates discretely lists and sells more Main Street businesses than any other brokerage in the state.

Michael is an accomplished negotiator who is passionate about serving New Mexico's diverse small business community and seeing the next generation build wealth for themselves and their families. Selling or buying a small business can be a stressful experience for the stakeholders involved. Through transparency, neutrality, and the flow of information, he builds trust among sellers and buyers and creates the space where they come together to determine where their interests intersect. Michael has a sophisticated grasp of the various funding pathways, is able to calm nerves, and come up with pragmatic solutions.

Michael's leadership of Sam Goldenberg & Associates culminates a lifetime of experience in transaction management, negotiations, finance, and business consulting. He spent over 25 years in Mergers & Acquisitions, led a network of commercial real estate brokerages, and co-founded a successful business consultancy with a portfolio of national and international clients. Michael is a graduate of Stanford and Harvard Law School.

EMAIL:

michael@samgoldenberg.com

PHONE:

(505) 820-0163

WEBSITE:

http://www.samgoldenberg.com

FACEBOOK:

https://www.facebook.com/SamGoldenbergandAssociates

PAUL SEMENOFF

CONVERSATION WITH PAUL SEMENOFF

■ **Paul, you are a business broker with The Capital Group. Tell us about your work and the people you help.**

Paul Semenoff: We're a general business brokerage, and many people don't even know that business brokers exist. When owners want to sell their businesses, they often go to real estate agents. While real estate agents can help you buy and sell homes, we can help you buy and sell businesses. We work with all types of businesses, from about $200,000 to $2 million and up.

■ **What questions do business owners have when contacting you for help?**

Paul Semenoff: Many times, they are checking their own motivation. The idea exists that it is hard to sell a business because it is tough to find buyers, but typically, the motivated heart of the seller has the true impact on selling a business. Their head might be in the business, but it's time to sell if their heart isn't. Business owners sell for various reasons, including health issues, retirement, relocation, or simply needing to raise more capital for an additional investment.

■ **Statistics show that a small percentage of businesses that go to market actually sell. Can you speak to this?**

Paul Semenoff: I recently read an article on www.bizbuysell.com that transitions are up 24% from last year and just about up to where they were in 2019 before Covid. So that's very encouraging.

■ **What happens when owners try to sell businesses on their own?**

Paul Semenoff: Sometimes, they attempt and are very successful if they are savvy business owners. Other times, they make that attempt and call us to help them through the process.

■ What mistakes do owners make that sabotage their success in selling?

Paul Semenoff: It's a matter of getting the business appropriately packaged. Financials must be in order, including profit and loss statements, tax returns, data about sales, and sales history. Banks will require these items to provide financing for a potential buyer. Inexperienced sellers often do not have these items prepared and organized. In that case, we encourage them to hold off on the sale and get everything together because 99% of what buyers want to know about your business is on paper. You will have much greater success when you have your documents in order.

■ As we are coming out of a pandemic and experiencing the "Great Resignation," is it a good time to buy and sell businesses?

Paul Semenoff: The short answer is, "It depends." Many businesses had great success during the pandemic. So there are certainly businesses that are "pandemic-proof" or "recession-proof." But generally, the best time to sell a business is when it is on the up when sales are increasing. When it's declining, it is very difficult. It's a lot like the stock market - buy low, sell high.

■ Paul, what inspired you to get started in this field?

Paul Semenoff: It's very rewarding because many reasons for selling a business are centered around the seller. Perhaps they want to enjoy their retirement or spend more time with their family and children. So it's very nice to help them close a deal. It's fantastic to see business owners be able to fulfill all their goals upon starting the business. We love to be a part of helping them sell for a profit.

I was in the culinary business for many years and worked for a large foodservice distributor in business development and sales management. So I do have a bit of a niche in restaurants; I love restaurant people. I have a good understanding there, and though it can be challenging, I really enjoy working with that market segment.

■ Is there anything else you would like to share?

Paul Semenoff: Business owners need to start thinking about a plan for selling the business as soon as they open their doors. There are many things they can do over the years to prepare for a successful sale, so when the time comes, they're ready. Keep good books, tax returns, profit and loss statements, and inventory. Always think about what a buyer would want if they came in and purchased your business. What is the next thing you can do to take your business to the next level? Buyers are always interested in improvement. So always have something in the pipeline that you can do next to be more profitable, which can be shared with the buyer at the time of sale.

■ **How can people find you, connect with you, and learn more?**

Paul Semenoff: You can reach me directly at 530-906-3441. My email is paul@thecapitalgrp.com. We have offices in Northern California, East Tennessee, and Idaho. We can help people buy and sell businesses nationwide.

PAUL SEMENOFF

Broker/Member of International
Business Brokers Association

The Capital Group

Paul Semenoff has over 35 years of experience in the business sales world as a business owner, manager, and Broker. Paul is a member of the International Association of Business Brokers (IBBA) and the California Association Of Business Brokers (CABB) and holds real estate broker's licenses in California, Idaho, and Tennessee. His firm, The Capital Group, does business nationwide.

Paul is a culinary school graduate who has worked as a Chef in some of California's finest restaurants and has spent over 20 years in sales management and business development for Sysco, the nation's largest foodservice distributor. Paul enjoys helping all types of business people, but with his background, he especially loves to help restaurant owners meet their business objectives.

Paul and his wife of 40 years reside in beautiful East Tennessee, where he enjoys the outdoors, playing bass and guitar, and oil painting.

EMAIL:

paul@thecapitalgrp.com

PHONE:

530-906-3441

WEBSITE:

www.thecapitalgrp.com

PHILIP
WEBB

CONVERSATION
WITH PHILIP WEBB

■ **Philip, you are a business broker with Transworld Business Advisors of North Central Alabama. Tell us about your work and the people you help.**

Philip Webb: My job as an intermediary is to act as an advisor first. It is my responsibility to source owners looking to sell their businesses. We often work with sellers who want to pass their businesses down to second and third generations. We analyze their business metrics, complete an evaluation, and confidentially network the opportunity to a wide range of qualified buyers in our network. We try to create competition for the seller's business by working with multiple potential buyers. Then we assist the seller with negotiations while helping them facilitate a closing. It really comes down to helping business owners achieve their goal of selling their business to the right type of buyer.

■ Do owners know where to start when they are ready to sell their businesses?

Philip Webb: Many of them don't. That's where we come in to help educate them. We often talk to people a year before selling the business to develop an exit strategy. Whether you own a Main Street or Sub-Middle Market Business, an exit strategy is essential. We help develop that strategy, and when they are ready to sell, we help them through the process too.

■ What types of things make businesses less sellable?

Philip Webb: The issue with small businesses is that they don't run themselves. The owner does much of the work, and that key person will typically need to be replaced upon sale. A potential buyer's primary concern is always, "How do I replace the owner? How do I make their mousetrap better, and how do I mitigate risk when purchasing a business?"

■ How are business intermediaries valuable to business owners?

Philip Webb: A business owner must constantly work on their day-to-day operations, handling clients, and customer support. It will be a daunting task if they try to sell their business independently. The process involves evaluating your business and looking at it through a general SWOT analysis (strengths, weaknesses, opportunities, and threats). Then you also need to work directly with buyers to explain the strengths and weaknesses of the business. Depending on your business type, trying to sell on your own could take up a good portion of your time when you need to be focusing on running the company. Working with an intermediary takes all of that stress off your shoulders. In addition, an intermediary acts as a third-party working with the buyer *and* the seller. We help sellers achieve their goal of selling the business while ensuring the buyers will be satisfied with their next opportunities.

■ Are there myths and misconceptions about selling a business?

Philip Webb: Many sellers are very proud of their businesses and don't understand where valuations and multiples come into play when evaluating a business. They look at their historical cash flow and revenue and assume it will be worth much more than a buyer would actually be willing to pay. This isn't like selling a house where you renovate, pick out curtains, and stage it for buyers. Selling a business is based on pure recurring revenues and ensuring the cash flow supports what you are trying to sell the business for while mitigating risk for the buyer. Each buyer has a different model and goal when purchasing a business. One buyer may have a completely different set of expectations of valuation of the seller's business compared to another. That is where a business intermediary can provide analysis to both parties to substantiate the valuation or price of the business while reflecting how the potential business can support the buyer's goals and objectives.

■ **As we are coming out of a pandemic, is it a good time to buy and sell businesses? What have you seen in your market?**

Philip Webb: When the pandemic started, the market was very flat. There was a lot of uncertainty out there. Lenders went into hiding and were only helping business owners with PPP and EIDL loans. Now that the sellers have gotten through the pandemic and figured out how to be more efficient, we see stronger support from buyers and lenders for acquisitions. We still would like to see more since there are way more buyers than sellers right now, and there are still good businesses out there that could be selling. They are just trying to manage the uncertainty. But as far as the economy, we see many strengths depending on the industry.

■ **Philip, what inspired you to get started in this field?**

Philip Webb: I was a corporate and commercial banker for 27 years. So I've always helped small businesses when it had to do with assisting them in acquisitions. And I've worked directly in all facets of the banking world. So it just made sense for me to be involved in a business where I'm actually helping owners acquire businesses or owners who want to sell their businesses. I've built a team of about three different agents with very successful backgrounds. It's just been fun. It's my business, so I enjoy running it, and there is still a corporate function that enables us to offer more services while educating clients. So we can be as big as we want to be or be as small as we want to be. We can empower people and move quickly, which is very helpful, especially in the corporate world.

■ Is there anything else you would like to share?

Philip Webb: The key to selling a business is preparation. Never try to sell when you're down - always sell when you see excellent results. Surround yourself with a team of people such as your accountant, attorney, and a business intermediary to help prepare your information and support you in selling your business. As intermediaries, we serve as project managers to herd everyone together while striving to meet either the seller's or the buyer's goals and objectives.

- ## How can people find you, connect with you, and learn more?

Philip Webb: My website is www.tworld.com/birminghamsw. You can also email me at pwebb@tworld.com. I am happy to help educate both buyers and sellers.

PHILIP WEBB

President/Principal Broker

Transworld Business Advisors of North Central Alabama

Transworld Business Advisors of North Central Alabama offers franchise consulting, franchise development, and business brokerage services to help business owners identify and capitalize on franchise and transactional successes. They assist clients with business valuation, sales assistance, and impartial brokerage services.

Philip Webb is the President and Principal Broker specializing in business advisory and brokerage services for Main Street and middle-market businesses. Before purchasing this business, he was a senior commercial and corporate banker with 27 years of experience in all aspects of commercial banking and/or commercial credit analysis. Philip is effective in building profitable relationships while experienced in generating professional consultation for superior results while consistently retaining clients.

Philip has expertise in business advisory for selling a business and experience in assisting buyers in analyzing opportunities and structuring deals. He has experience structuring and financing facilities such as commercial owner-occupied real estate, commercial investor-owned real estate projects, SBA programs, C&I lines of credit, term, and equipment financing. Philip has additional experience providing lending, Treasury Management, and Commercial solutions to SIC code industries for health care and agriculture companies coupled with Public Institutions and Non-profit companies.

Affiliated with IBBA, MAS, BNI, CCIM, and RMA

Commercial Training: Advanced RMA training and certification, Advanced Lending for Key Industry Segmentation and Commercial Real Estate, Financial Accounting Review; Financial Analysis Review I-4; Cash Flow Analysis; Loan Structuring; Pricing; Managing Risk, Managing Problem Loans; RMA Commercial Lending for Municipalities, Non-Profits, Churches, Schools, and Hospitals.

EMAIL:
pwebb@tworld.com

PHONE:
205-218-0901

WEBSITE:
https://www.tworld.com/locations/birminghamsw/

LINKEDIN:
https://www.linkedin.com/in/philip-webb/

FACEBOOK:
https://www.facebook.com/tbanorthcentralal

BIZBUYSELL:
https://www.bizbuysell.com/business-broker/philip-webb/
transworld-business-advisors-of-north-central-alabama/30713/

PATRICK COLLINS

CONVERSATION WITH PATRICK COLLINS

■ **Patrick, you are the founder of www. calbizvalue.com and a business broker with Sunbelt Business Brokers and Advisors. Tell us about your work and the people you help.**

Patrick Collins: The core elements of what I do involve helping business owners and buyers value businesses in a near-term look, determine marketability, and perform sales marketing tasks. If a business is not currently at a value the owner is satisfied with, I also provide advisory services to help them build to the desired exit value.

■ **Do owners know where to begin when it comes to selling a business?**

Patrick Collins: Many of them don't. A significant segment of the industry now is the baby boomers. They have run and built great businesses over 30 or 35 years. They've never sold a business and never bought one. Once they approach retirement, they realize they didn't build the business to exit. So it's an element of their planning that isn't handled early enough.

■ How far in advance should an owner prepare for the sale of their business?

Patrick Collins: Regardless of your age or how long you have owned the business, you should be planning everything you do based upon an exit, whether five, ten or twenty-five years down the road. But having two or three years to pull yourself together and be ready to go to market is ideal. Many owners are aware they need to have good, clean books, but not from the perspective of a possible exit. Start early and look at things often from an exit perspective.

■ As we are coming out of a pandemic, is it a good time to buy or sell a business? What have you seen in your market?

Patrick Collins: Obviously, restaurants were impacted negatively. On the other hand, some businesses deemed essential did better during Covid and had a different set of demands. For example, if you were a plastic manufacturer and pivoted to making those screens we all faced for the next two years, you did really well. So there's a variety of responses through the Covid period. But the overriding one for many people was, "Okay, we get one of these events about every ten years, and I don't want to go through the next one. So how do I prepare myself to get sold over the next few years before that next big event?"

■ **Statistics show that as many as 80% of businesses that go to market never sell. What are some reasons for this?**

Patrick Collins: Most of them have to do with pricing. What you think your business is worth and what the market will bear can be relatively far apart. A key component of that is: How financeable is it? You need to have a realistic market value that the market will bear instead of focusing on what you want or need. We use the most probable selling price model, which isn't an appraisal, but what we think the market will bear. It's based on market comparables in sales and revenues. So it gives business owners a realistic "today" value. They may disagree with it, which is fine. But then it's probably not ready to go to market until the owner accepts a realistic price.

■ **Is there still opportunity in niches that were affected negatively by Covid?**

Patrick Collins: There is definitely opportunity. But if you try to build on a brand that was there before Covid, it is essential to understand if it was Covid that hurt the brand. What did their sales look like two to four years before Covid? Many businesses were on their way out regardless. But Covid kind of pushed those businesses over the edge real quick. They couldn't adjust or pivot because they didn't have the financial wherewithal to push through. In the restaurant industry, it was delivery or curbside service. So there are certainly opportunities. In many cases, it just might be starting up and over and not trying to rebuild a brand that was hurt during the pandemic.

■ Is funding readily available in today's market?

Patrick Collins: A lot of business owners got PPP and EIDL loans. Depending on how those were handled, it can put another pause on exit and refinance. But most owners with PPP loans can work through them and get them forgiven. After the workload dropped on the SBA by the PPP and EIDL programs, the SBA is back to its traditional programs and back into the market. As a business broker, I can go to the SBA, have them look at a business, and have the business pre-approved subject to the buyer. That makes it much more saleable. But the opportunity still involves asking, "Where was this business before Covid, and where can I take it after?" Fundamentals are still important. For a simple example, if the business was in a lousy location before Covid, a PPP loan could not improve its location.

■ Patrick, what inspired you to get started in this field?

Patrick Collins: I've kind of been doing it all of my professional life, but not on a platform like this. I spent 20 years in commercial real estate, and there's real estate involved all the time with what I do now. I was also involved in the economic development field for a while, working with businesses looking to relocate. Then along the way, I did consulting work in between various formal roles, helping owners get their businesses on track. I wasn't doing this to get the business sold per se, but, in effect, I was helping them prepare for better outcomes.

I owned a business for ten years, and when I sold it, the brokerage owner called me and said, "Hey, have you ever thought about doing what I do?" As I thought about it, I realized I had been doing it all along, just not with that particular "broker" hat on.

■ Is there anything else you would like to share with business owners thinking about selling in today's economy?

Patrick Collins: I really want to emphasize focusing on fundamentals. Those need to be in place regardless of opportunity, lack of opportunity, up market, or down market. Evaluating a business during Covid, we look at the history of a business and can consider, is it entirely back, or did Covid take it out? Was there flexibility during Covid? Is the risk higher or lower as the business comes out of Covid? What is the industry trend? Is it improving, or as with the buggy whip manufacturing, is it clearly not "keeping up" with all the changes in the market? So you need to understand what is happening in your industry and what type of buyer will be interested in buying your business. If the daily headlines are about your industry failing, it will be a tough sell. But again, there can be roll-ups and opportunities in that scenario too. Focusing on fundamentals was important before Covid, during Covid, and today.

■ How can people find you, connect with you, and learn more?

Patrick Collins: A phone call or text is the quickest way. My number is 661-342-3436. It is completely confidential, and I am the only one answering or picking up messages. My direct email is patrick.collins@sunbeltnetwork.com, and you can always reach out on LinkedIn!

PATRICK COLLINS

California Broker DRE#1417794, Agent #00753204

Business Broker - Sunbelt Business Brokers and Advisors

Founder - www.calbizvalue.com

Patrick's professional experience includes 20 years in commercial real estate (CBRE), six years in economic development (Kern EDC, a public-private partnership), two years in engineering/planning (Quad Knopf), several years in advisory/consulting, and ten years as owner/CEO in the account recovery/collection industry (H P Sears-sold 2019). Patrick is also highly engaged in community activities, including serving on the boards of Rotary, Mid State Development (SBA), New Advances for People with Disabilities (NAPD), and the California State University Business School, and is a frequent guest on the Moneywise Financial Advisors radio show.

Patrick's experience, in conjunction with the Sunbelt Network, provides a wide array of tools to businesses—to assist in the purchase, sale, or growth of a business.

For advisory (growth, strategy, or exit planning), or transactional service (buy or sell), call or email for a complimentary consultation to discuss your interests and needs!

EMAIL:

patrick.collins@sunbeltnetwork.com

PHONE:

661-342-3436

WEBSITE:

https://www.sunbeltnetwork.com/bakersfield-ca/

OTHER:

https://calbizvalue.com/

RICHARD S. WAXMAN

RICHARD S. WAXMAN

CONVERSATION WITH RICHARD S. WAXMAN

■ **Richard, you are the Managing Partner of M&A Business Advisors. Tell us about your work and the people you help.**

Richard S. Waxman: I work primarily with sellers through a seller representation agreement. These sellers have either founded or purchased a business, run it for two or three decades, and are ready to retire and take the next step in their lives. Though they know a lot about their particular business, they often don't know a lot about the fundamentals of financing, marketing, and negotiating the sale of a business. So I work on a retainer with a commission kicker at the end for success, 100% commission, or sometimes strictly hourly. That is one segment of my business.

The other piece is working with people looking to purchase a business. They have excellent experience in business management, but they have no idea how to find a business and secure it on their own. So I get hired to be a buyer representative. And as part of that, I do a search acquisition, where I attempt to find businesses that are not currently on the market but could be on the market because a motivated buyer is out there. Typically, all we have to do is approach the owner. So I work on the same principles here, occasionally straight commission, but more often a combination of commission and hourly consultation, or strictly hourly. So that's what I do. A big part of that is helping people value their businesses to make a judgment about a fair asking price for their company.

■ Are there myths and misconceptions about selling a business?

Richard S. Waxman: Well, I won't call it a myth; I'll call it a phenomenon. Sellers often think their business will bring in a higher price than the market is willing to pay, and that's pretty natural. There's some degree of misinformation out there about how businesses are priced. From time to time, I talk with rather sophisticated people who believe that businesses are priced based on just gross sales. And with very few exceptions, that's not the case. It's a measure of profitability and so-called "free cash" flow. And then each industry has a certain comparable multiple times that number, which is typically how you value a business. So I'd say one common phenomenon with sellers is that they have an impression that their business will be priced much higher than it ultimately should be. We do a valuation report and provide 25 or so comparable sales, a discounted cash flow analysis, and an asset valuation. We do a blended average of these items, with heavier weight on comparable sales. We are always trying to educate sellers.

The other common phenomenon in dealing with sellers is they have a preconceived notion of the ideal buyer for the business, which is relatively common. And there's nothing wrong with that, but it's important to open the marketing to as many possible buyer sources as possible because you never know who might be the best buyer. We market businesses very discreetly, and it's kind of a "come one, come all" if the buyers are qualified.

■ **As we are coming out of a pandemic, is this a good time to buy or sell a business? What have you seen in your market?**

Richard S. Waxman: 2021 was a good year, and 2022 has continued to be strong. Many external factors are involved. Interest rates are going up now. As a country, we had negative GDP in the first quarter, but I'd say it's still an excellent time to sell. Although interest rates are up, they're still relatively lower than historically. So people can still borrow money through their corporate lines of credit or, if they're individual buyers, through bank finance programs. So I think people have to decide not just their timing from a market point of view, but from a personal point of view, are they ready to sell? Do they have a plan post-closing for what they will do with their life? So if it's the right time on a personal basis, we can help them.

■ Richard, what inspired you to
get started in this field?

Richard S. Waxman: I came from a commercial real estate background. I started many years ago in industrial sales and leasing. That morphed into general commercial sales and leasing. I happened to get a listing that was a successful breakfast and lunch restaurant. It had two apartments upstairs, and we had to find a buyer with the money to purchase the real estate and the background and experience to run the restaurant. So it was two separate transactions because real property is real property. And this was personal property. So it was a different set of legal listings. In any case, we found a buyer, which led me to sell other restaurants, independent of the property in most cases. Then I began selling businesses in general. Now I've been doing it since the late 90s.

■ Is there anything else you would like to share?

Richard S. Waxman: I think having a quality relationship with a qualified business intermediary is essential. That means there must be trust, respect, and even a modicum of affection. The intermediary must have not only really good knowledge, which is critical but also excellent communication skills and the ability to work effectively with other people. They need to be able to work with other advisors to the seller or buyer, such as attorneys and CPAs. So make sure you have a really solid relationship with that party. And it isn't always someone willing to work the least expensively. If you save some dollars up front, you may pay back dollars later.

■ How can people find you, connect with you, and learn more?

Richard S. Waxman: If you Google "Richard Waxman, Business Intermediary or Business Broker," I will come up. My direct line is 415-515-3487. You can email me at rwaxman@mabusinessadvisors.com.

.

RICHARD S. WAXMAN

Managing Partner

M&A Business Advisors - San Francisco

Richard is one of six partners in a California-based merger and acquisition consultation and brokerage firm. He brings over thirty years of background, knowledge, and experience to this process. Starting in the real estate industry as a commercial broker, he began selling restaurants that were housed in mixed-use property. That morphed into general business brokerage and has resulted in the sale of over one hundred transactions involving various companies. His knowledge of the ins and outs of the buying and selling process has been enhanced by his decade-long tenure as managing broker of one of California's largest general brokerage firm's San Francisco office. There he supervised a dozen other brokers, building the office from the ground up to be the top firm in San Francisco.

He has been a presenter at the California Association of Business Brokers and the International Association of Business Brokers annual productivity conventions.

Among services currently available to clients are opinion of value reports, contingency representation of sellers, and hourly fee consultation engagements for both buyers and sellers.

References and letters of recommendation are available upon request.

EMAIL:
rwaxman@mabusinessadvisors.com

PHONE:
(415) 515-3487

WEBSITE:
www.mabusinessadvisors.com

BIO:
https://www.mabusinessadvisors.com/richardwaxman

ROXANNE REID

ROXANNE REID

CONVERSATION WITH ROXANNE REID

■ **Roxanne, you are the founder of
Capital Valuations. Tell us about your
work and the people you help.**

Roxanne Reid: I work as a business broker. As business owners approach me, I find that many of them don't know where to start when it comes to selling their business. They have questions like, "How do I start the process? What is my company worth?" There are many moving parts to selling a business. Being ready to sell is a key part of maximizing all those hard years of work you put into your business. So, my ideal customer is somebody thinking about selling, and they're about three to five years from actually taking that step. We can use those years to get things in place. The truth is that every business should be ready to sell every day. Run your business like it's for sale because you never know when you might exit or under what terms. You might plan for retirement, but other life events happen. Disability, divorce, dissolving partnerships, distress, and death are all factors that can trigger an exit outside of retirement. Exit planning is just good business planning.

■ Where do owners begin when it comes to selling their business?

Roxanne Reid: Start with where you are. It's really as simple as that. Where are you financially? Where are you with your management team? Helping owners answer these questions is the reason I launched Capital Valuations. Part of my business is to help people get started by providing a valuation of their business. As a Certified Exit Planning Advisor with the Exit Planning Institute, I have supporting materials for business owners. Every business owner will want to know three things: profit gap, value gap, and wealth gap.

Regarding the profit and value gap, many business owners focus on growth, growth, growth. But the value of a business isn't only the revenue it produces. What if you have a $10 million business, but you're losing $12 million? So it's not about revenue and growth, growth, growth. What are you doing within the business itself? What makes your business attractive to a buyer?

I work with several different programs to prepare valuation reports. One of the things I do is go through your company and determine what would make it first in class. What could you do with that extra cash flow if you were to take the revenue you're making now and close the value and profit gaps? How does it impact the value of your

business? So the reports I go through with business owners cover 400 data points and five key drivers of business. When we're done with that, we will be able to tell you where your profit gaps are, what the key drivers are, and where to focus.

You don't want to major in the minors; you don't want to focus on something that will give you a small return. You want to focus on what will provide you with the biggest bang for your buck, especially if you look at three to five years before you exit. Being able to "see" and track a 40% or 50% increase in the value of your business is a huge motivator for owners. Being ready to sell, knowing your key drivers, and having processes in place will increase the multiples that can be applied for the industry. That's what I bring to the table; today's valuation, tomorrow's next steps, and the exit you planned for at the price you deserve.

■ Are there myths and misconceptions about selling a business?

Roxanne Reid: There are some things I see time and time again, and it's kind of sad. Business owners often think the value of their business is what they want from it. And as I mentioned, there are gaps. And that wealth gap is a key piece. So when they are ready to retire or exit their business, they often have a number in their head they think they need for retirement. All of a sudden, that's the value of their business. In reality, that is their personal wealth gap. And maybe the business can fill that gap, or perhaps it can't. The value of your business is what someone is willing to pay for it, not what you *feel* it is worth.

■ Roxanne, what inspired you to get started in this field?

Roxanne Reid: I retired two years ago, just before the start of Covid, from a corporate role. I had plans to go into business with my daughter, and suddenly those plans went out the window.

Picking up on an earlier career of being a florist, we were going to be wedding planners, and I would be doing the design work. She would be working with the young brides because she's in that age group. We thought it would be a nice balance. We had already gotten off to a great start; after promoting the business for three weeks, we already had 18 weddings booked. Then Covid. At this point, I'd already retired and thought, "What am I going to do with myself?" I had always been the "go-to" person in whatever business I was in and the one who connected people.

Quite frankly, I was lonely and isolated. My daughter was in a different province, separated by distance and Covid rules. I needed to feel connected and get outside of my own four walls. I started getting into social media like LinkedIn and Facebook and grew my connections and followings by the thousands. Through LinkedIn, I saw someone locally with the job title of "business broker." And it was like the universe was coming at me. I knew this was what I wanted to do! So I joined the company as an assistant. Since I didn't have a lot of background in the industry and they weren't sure I had what it took, they had me take a personality profile. It was no surprise to me that I was a 96% match! From there, I jumped in with both feet and have just been taking courses, building my LinkedIn network, and following great thought leaders already in the industry. That led me to find the CEPA designation (Certified Exit Planning Advisor). I received that designation, completed coursework to be a Certified Business Broker, and completed the Mastery of Negotiations Program through Harvard Business School online.

I'm currently enrolled in the Mergers and Acquisitions program at Columbia Business School online with plans to be a Certified International Valuations Expert. I'm constantly building upon my knowledge and expertise. I do this because I value the trust my clients place in me. I always want to be able to give the very best advice and offer supporting resources for my clients. I've had a tremendous first year, growing organically by my initial clients who referred friends and business colleagues. I've learned so much along the way and used this to incorporate new offerings such as the valuations piece and lending services to round out what clients are looking for. I'm loving every minute of it.

- ## How can people find you, connect with you, and learn more?

Roxanne Reid: You can find me at www.capital-valuations.com. The website is a dynamic source of information with constant updates and new additions. Email: info@capital-valuations.com or reach me by phone at 506-238-0133 or 1-800-810-7085.

ROXANNE REID, CEPA, CLU

Founder

Capital Valuations by the Reid Group

Roxanne Reid, CEPA, CLU, is a professional business broker with over 38 years of experience in finance, business management, and marketing. She is a Harvard-trained Master Negotiator and a proud International Business Brokers Association (IBBA) member. She has completed all the courses for the prestigious Certified Business Intermediary (CBI) designation, the industry's highest recognition for an experienced and dedicated business broker.

As a Certified Exit Planning Advisor (CEPA), she is committed to helping business owners maximize the value of their business and ensuring buyers are getting the best value for their investment.

Roxanne values the trust clients place in her capable hands and rewards that trust with expert advice and results. Her genuine interest in her clients shows in her attention to detail and the level of care she provides to see businesses successfully bought and sold.

EMAIL:
info@capital-valuations.com

PHONE:
1-506-238-0133 or 1-800-810-7085

WEBSITE:
www.capital-valuations.com

LINKEDIN:
www.linkedin.com/in/roxanne-reid

ABOUT THE PUBLISHER

Mark Imperial is a Best-Selling Author, Syndicated Business Columnist, Syndicated Radio Host, and internationally recognized Stage, Screen, and Radio Host of numerous business shows spotlighting leading experts, entrepreneurs, and business celebrities.

His passion is to discover noteworthy business owners, professionals, experts, and leaders who do great work and share their stories and secrets to their success with the world on his syndicated radio program titled "Remarkable Radio."

Mark is also the media marketing strategist and voice for some of the world's most famous brands. You can hear his voice over the airwaves weekly on Chicago radio and worldwide on iHeart Radio.

Mark is a Karate black belt; teaches Muay Thai and Kickboxing; loves Thai food, House Music, and his favorite TV shows are infomercials.

Learn more:

www.MarkImperial.com
www.BooksGrowBusiness.com